Simple Machines

Levers

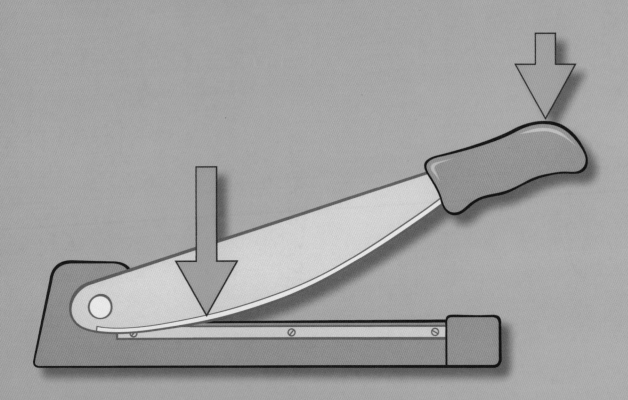

Chris Oxlade

FRANKLIN WATTS
LONDON·SYDNEY

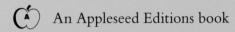 An Appleseed Editions book

First published in 2007 by Franklin Watts

Franklin Watts
338 Euston Road, London NW1 3BH

Franklin Watts Australia
Hachette Children's Books
Level 17/207 Kent St, Sydney, NSW 2000

© 2007 Appleseed Editions

Created by Appleseed Editions Ltd,
Well House, Friars Hill, Guestling,
East Sussex TN35 4ET

Designed by Helen James
Edited by Mary-Jane Wilkins
Artwork by Bill Donohoe

ISBN 978 0 7496 7566 0

Dewey Classification: 621.8' 11

A CIP catalogue for this book is available from the British Library.

Photo credits
page 5 Lito C. Uyan/Corbis; 6 Gaetano/Corbis; 9 Colin Garratt; Milepost 92 1/2/Corbis;
11 Ole Graf/Zefa/Corbis; 12 First Light/Corbis; 15 Roy McMahon/Corbis; 18 Jeremy
Hardie/Zefa/Corbis; 19 Roy McMahon/Corbis; 20 Robert Llewellyn/Zefa/Corbis;
21 Courtesy of Hunter Engineering Company; 22 Enzo & Paolo Ragazzini/Corbis;
26 Patrick Johns/Corbis; 28 Mika/Zefa/Corbis

Printed in China

Franklin Watts is a division of Hachette Children's Books

Contents

What is a simple machine?

A simple machine is something that helps you do a job. We use simple machines to help us every day. Here are some simple machines you might have at home.

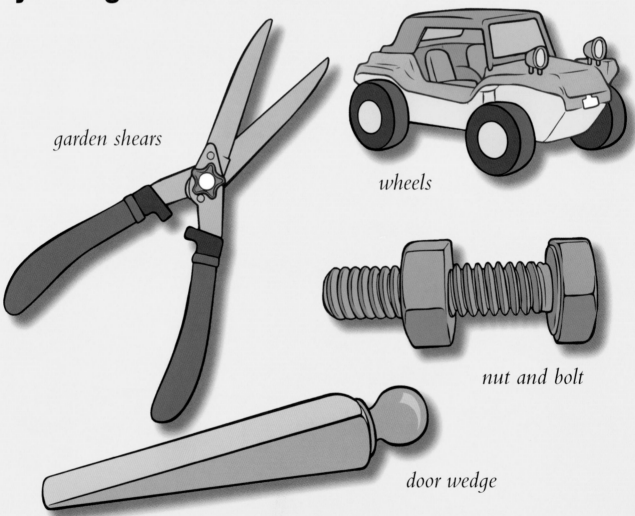

garden shears

wheels

nut and bolt

door wedge

This book is about simple machines called levers. A bottle opener is a lever. The opener makes it easy to pull off a metal bottle top. Door handles, scissors, spanners and nut crackers are all levers, too.

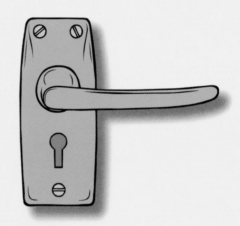

Pulling up on a bottle opener pulls off the bottle top.

Pushes and pulls

You push or pull on a lever to make it work. When you push or pull, the lever makes a push or a pull too. Scientists call all pushes and pulls forces.

These are wire cutters. When you push on the handles, the blades cut through the wire.

We show pushes and pulls with arrows. The arrow points in the direction the force is pushing or pulling. The longer the arrow the bigger the push or pull is.

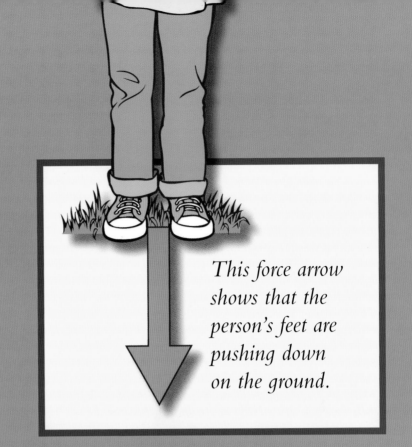

This force arrow shows that the person's feet are pushing down on the ground.

Red arrows show pushes and pulls.

Blue arrows show movement.

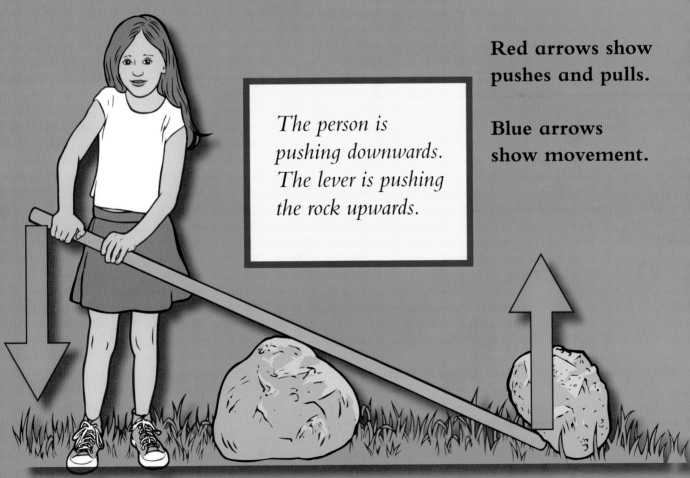

The person is pushing downwards. The lever is pushing the rock upwards.

How a lever works

A lever is a long, narrow piece of material, such as a metal bar or a wooden stick.

A lever can make a push or a pull larger or smaller. It can also change the direction of a push or pull. One part of a lever always stays still. This is the pivot.

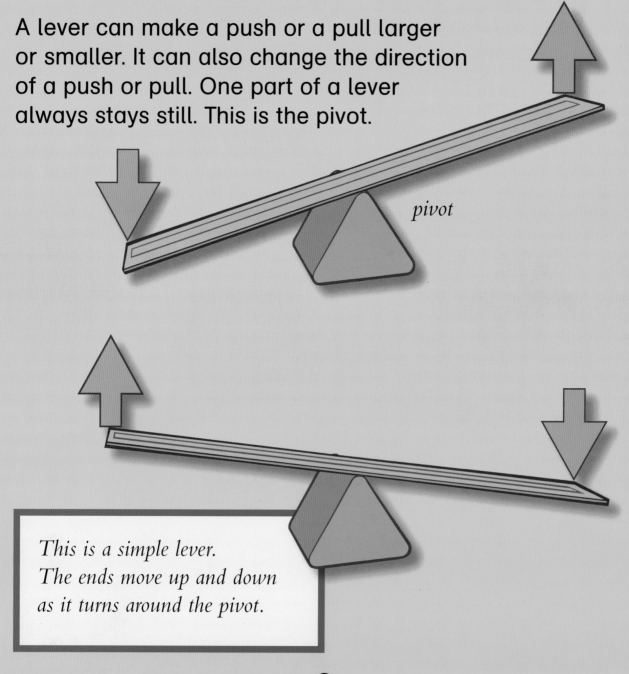

pivot

This is a simple lever. The ends move up and down as it turns around the pivot.

These levers are making the men's pushes larger. They do up the bolts very tightly.

These tweezers have two levers joined together. They make a push smaller so you can pick up delicate things.

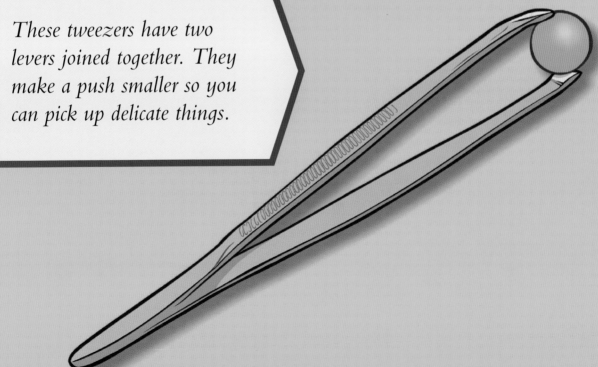

9

Lifting with levers

We use levers to help lift heavy things.

A crowbar is a long metal bar with bent ends. We use a crowbar to lift up concrete slabs or drain covers. A small push down on the bar lifts the heavy slab or cover.

When you push down on the crowbar, it lifts up the drain cover.

The curved end of the crowbar fits under the edge of the drain cover.

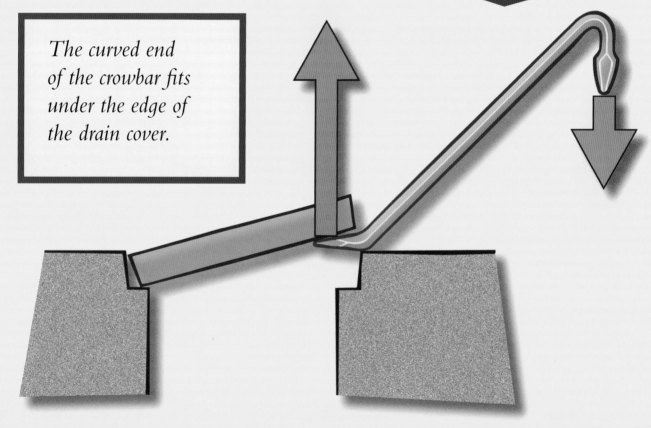

On a see-saw, the pivot is right in the middle.

A see-saw is a lever. When you sit on one end of a see-saw your weight pushes down on it. That pushes up the person at the other end.

A see-saw changes the direction of a push from down to up.

Turning with levers

We use levers to turn things.
A spanner turns nuts and bolts.

A spanner's handle is a lever.
The handle makes it easy to tighten
nuts and bolts, or to undo them.

*The spanner fits neatly
on to the top of the nut.*

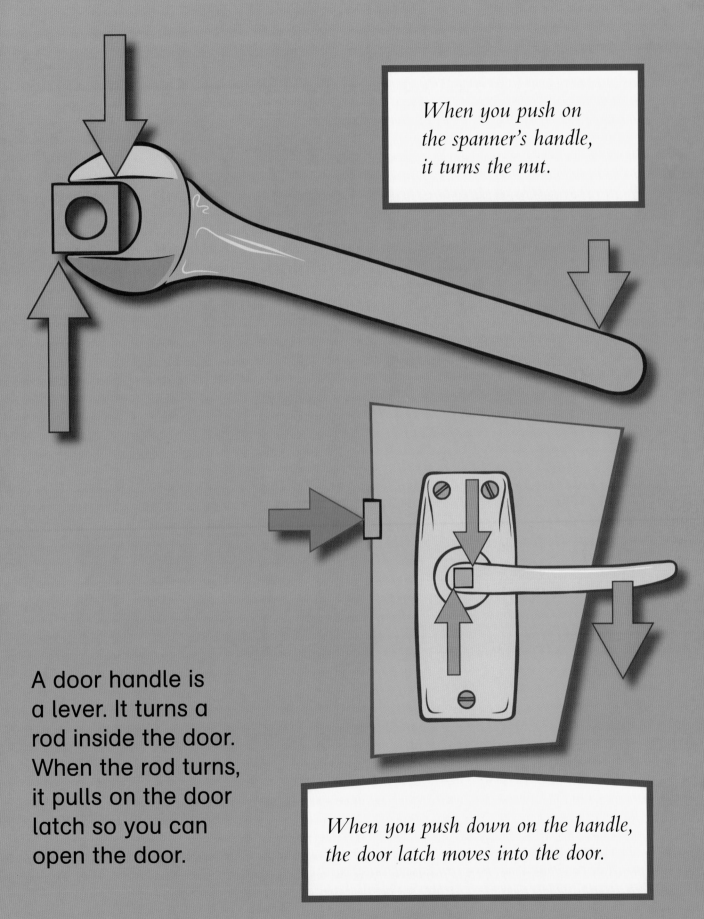

When you push on
the spanner's handle,
it turns the nut.

A door handle is
a lever. It turns a
rod inside the door.
When the rod turns,
it pulls on the door
latch so you can
open the door.

When you push down on the handle,
the door latch moves into the door.

Gripping with levers

**We use levers to grip things tightly.
A pair of pliers is a gripping tool.**

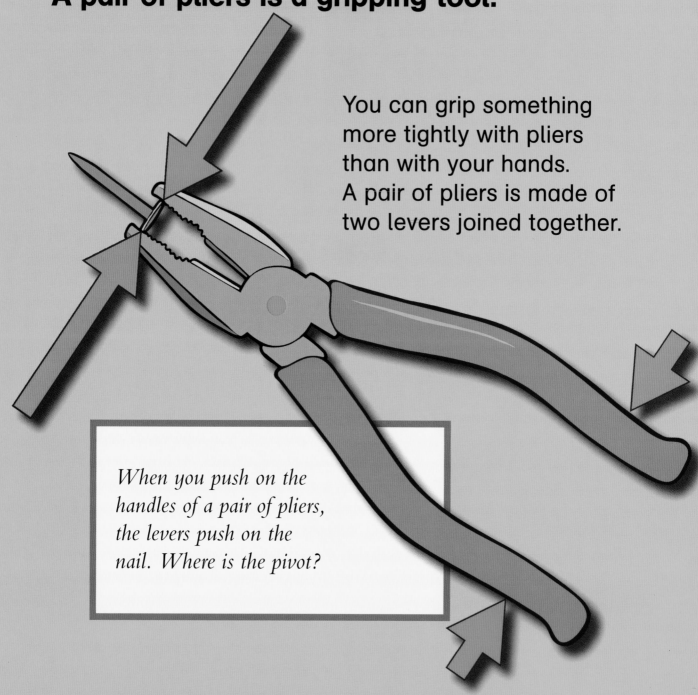

You can grip something
more tightly with pliers
than with your hands.
A pair of pliers is made of
two levers joined together.

*When you push on the
handles of a pair of pliers,
the levers push on the
nail. Where is the pivot?*

The two levers in a pair of tongs are joined at one end.

A pair of tongs is made up of two joined handles. Each handle is a lever. Squeezing the two handles together makes the ends of the levers move together to grip an object.

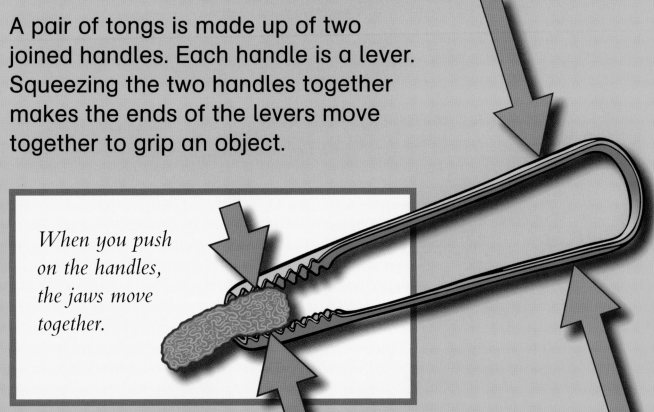

When you push on the handles, the jaws move together.

Cutting with levers

**We use levers to cut things.
A guillotine is a machine that cuts
paper. Its handle and blade are a lever.**

You press down on the handle.
The lever makes your push much bigger
so the blade slices through the paper.

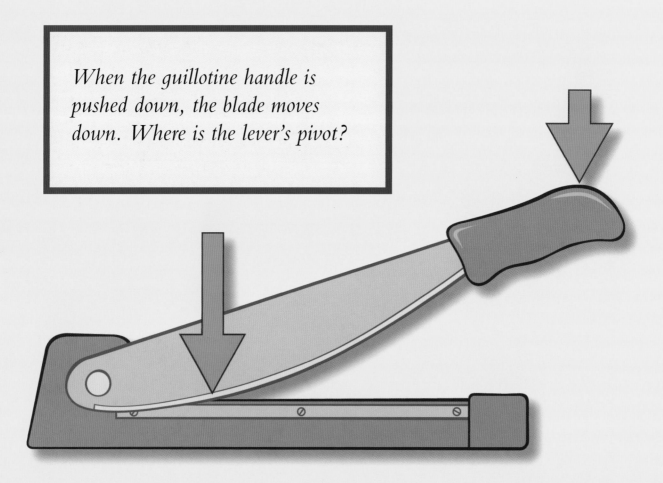

*When the guillotine handle is
pushed down, the blade moves
down. Where is the lever's pivot?*

A pair of bolt cutters is made of two handles joined together. Each handle is a lever. When you push the two handles together the levers make a bigger push. This makes the blades cut through thick metal.

When the handles are pushed together, the blades move together.

Bolt cutters have very long handles. This makes cutting metal easier.

Levers in machines

Complicated machines often use levers to work.

The brake handle on a bicycle is a lever.
Pulling on the handle makes the handle
pull a wire. The wire makes the brakes work.

*A bicycle's brake handle
is often called a brake lever.*

Some exercise machines have levers. Pulling or pushing on the lever is hard work. Making the push or pull is good exercise.

Pushing and pulling these levers exercises the arms.

A sailor steers a sailing boat with a rudder. The sailor moves the rudder from side to side with a lever called a tiller.

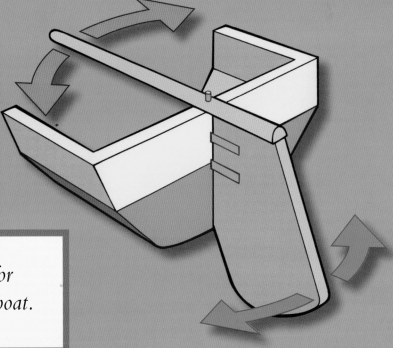

The tiller makes it easy for a sailor to steer a sailing boat.

More levers in machines

Many building machines use levers to work. A mechanical digger uses lots of levers.

This digger arm has two levers. Where are their pivots?

A digger's arm is made up of levers joined together. The levers are pushed and pulled by a hydraulic ram. This makes them move up and down. The rams are like the muscles in your arm.

There are levers inside a tractor's cab. The driver pushes and pulls on the levers to make parts of the tractor work.

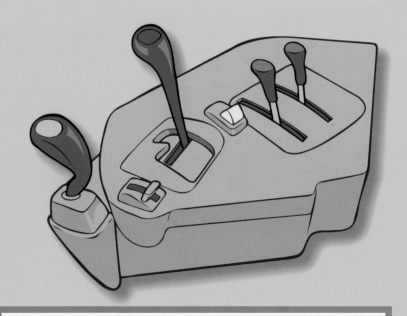

The levers let the driver work the heavy tractor with gentle pulls and pushes.

A scissor lift raises people and equipment up in the air. The platform is supported by lots of levers.

Why do you think this machine is called a scissor lift?

Levers in the past

People have been using levers for thousands of years.

The heavy baskets of stones pull down. This lifts up the water bucket.

This simple machine is called a shaduf.
It lifts water from a stream so it can be
poured on to a field to water growing crops.

Simple weighing machines use levers. The thing being weighed hangs on one end. Weights hang on the other end.

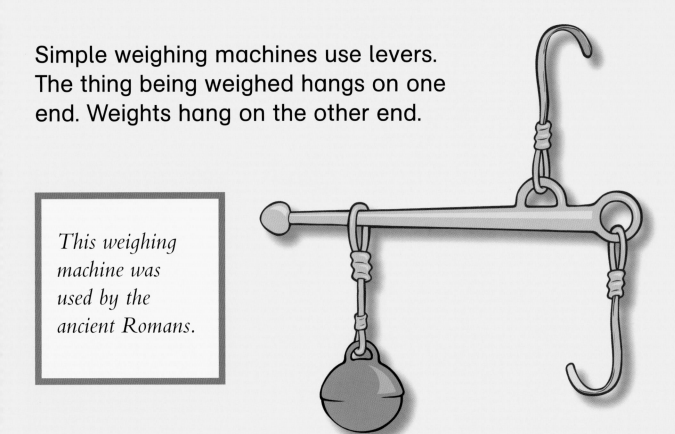

This weighing machine was used by the ancient Romans.

Levers were even used in battle. This machine is called a trebuchet (treb-u-shay). It used a lever to throw huge rocks at an enemy.

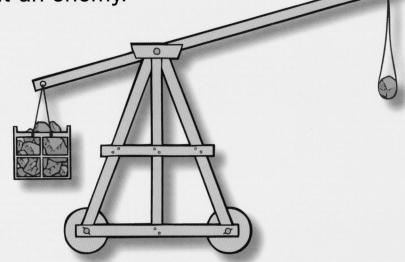

The lever on a trebuchet was moved by a huge load of rocks.

Lever fun

On the next four pages are some activities for you to do. They will help you to understand how levers work.

A LIFTING LEVER

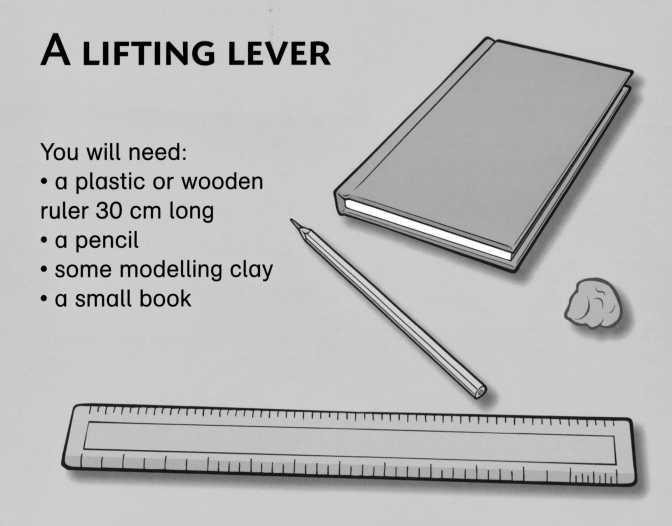

You will need:
• a plastic or wooden ruler 30 cm long
• a pencil
• some modelling clay
• a small book

1	Put the pencil on a table. Press a blob of modelling clay on to each end to stop the pencil moving.

2 Put the ruler on the pencil so that the 10 cm line is over the pencil.

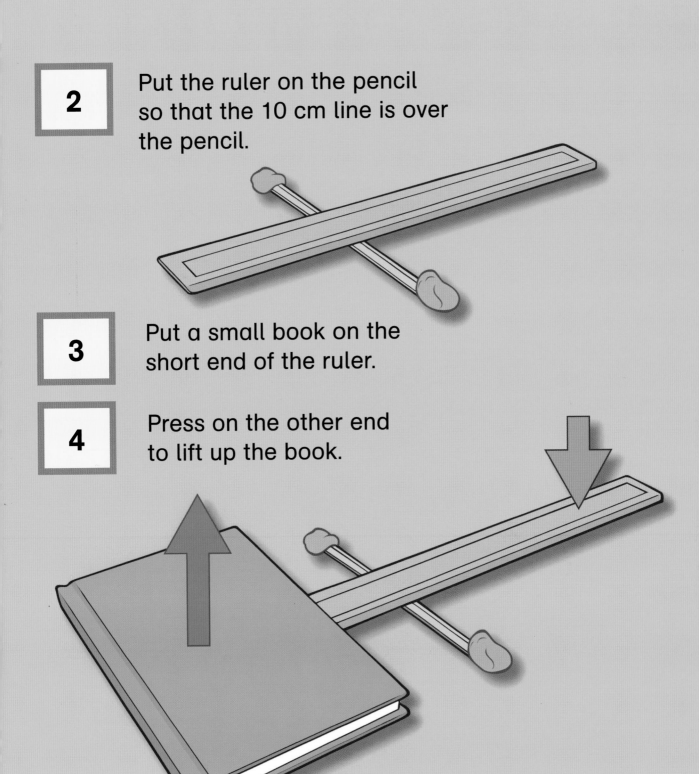

3 Put a small book on the short end of the ruler.

4 Press on the other end to lift up the book.

The lever (ruler) makes your push bigger. It makes it easy to lift the book.

A BROOM LEVER

You will need:
• a broom (or a strong stick such as a broom handle)
• a large plastic box
• some books

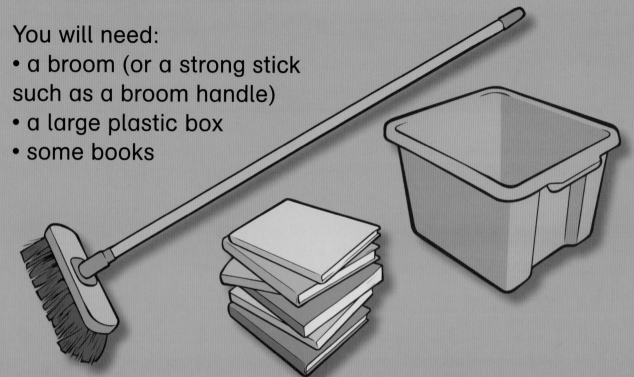

A gardener uses a fork as a lever to pull up a potato plant.

1 Put the books in the box to make the box heavy.

2 Try pushing the box along the floor. Remember how hard you have to push to move the box.

3 Put the box against a wall. Push the end of the broom handle behind the box.

4 Pull the other end of the handle away from the wall to move the box.

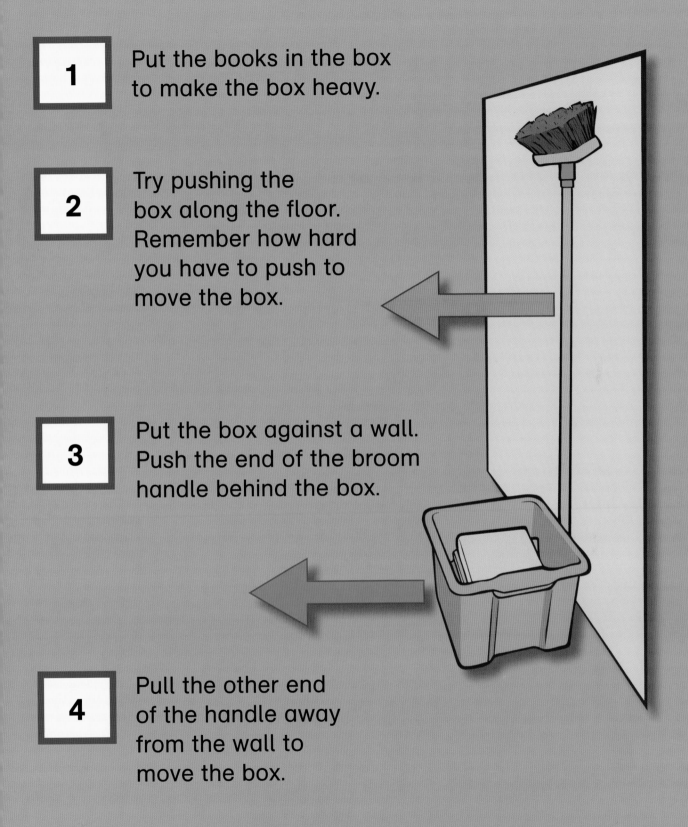

The broom works like a lever.
It makes it easier to move the box.

Spot the lever

Can you spot all the levers here?
Try to work out what each lever does.

Which part of this wheelbarrow is a lever?

Where is the lever here?
What job does it do?

Where do you pull on
this lever? What does
the lever pull on?

What is the lever
here? What makes
the lever move?

Answers are on page 32

29

Words to remember

bolt cutters
A machine made of two levers,
used for cutting through thick bolts.

crowbar
A long steel bar with a hook at one end.

forces
Pushes or pulls.

guillotine
A machine for cutting paper and card.

pivot
The place that a lever turns round.

pliers
A machine made of two levers,
used for gripping things tightly.

rudder
A flat piece of material on the back of a boat,
that is turned from side to side to steer the boat.

shaduf
A lever used to lift water from a well.

spanner
A lever used to turn a nut or bolt.

tiller
A lever used to turn the rudder of a boat
from side to side.

trebuchet
A machine used in the past by soldiers
for throwing rocks at an enemy.

wire cutters
A machine made of two levers, used
for cutting through wire.

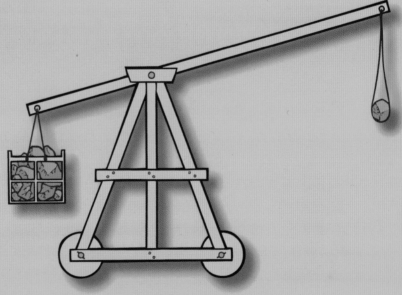

Index

Answers to pages 28-29
The long handles of a wheelbarrow are levers.
The red handle is a lever. Pulling it squeezes water from the sponge.
Pulling down on the hammer handle pulls out the nail.
Your arm is a lever! Your muscles move it.